Simplify to Serve

A Blueprint to Lead a Well-Run Nonprofit
Without Losing Your Sanity

CINDY WALTERS
MSSW, ACNP

Simplify to Serve: A Blueprint to Lead a Well-Run Nonprofit without Losing Your Sanity
Published by Wren Publishing House LLC
Denver, CO

ISBN: 979-8-218-09814-8
Nonprofit Organizations & Charities / Management & Leadership

Cover and interior design by Victoria Wolf, wolfdesignandmarketing.com, copyright owned by Cindy Walters LLC.

This publication is designed to provide accurate and authoritative information in regard to the subject matter covered. It is sold with the understanding that the publisher is not engaged in rendering legal, accounting, or other professional services. If legal advice or other expert assistance is required, the services of a competent professional person should be sought.

Praise for *Simplify to Serve*

"What a game-changer for small nonprofit executive directors! The author offers practical solutions to common challenges faced by nonprofits. The plain language and the step-by-step guides are simple to follow. I highly recommend *Simplify to Serve* to anyone looking to lead a more efficient and effective organization."

—Susan Tomlinson Schmidt, MPA, ACNP, Former National President, Nonprofit Leadership Alliance

"An excellent resource for nonprofit leaders seeking to streamline their operations and improve their effectiveness. The book is full of practical insights and actionable advice that make this book a must-read for anyone looking to lead a successful and sustainable nonprofit organization."

—Winn Jewett, CEO, BoardSpot

"As a seasoned nonprofit leader, I know firsthand how overwhelming the role of Executive Director can be. *Simplify to Serve* offers a breath of fresh air, providing practical tips and strategies for streamlining operations and creating a sustainable work-life balance. Cindy's passion for helping non-profit leaders truly thrive so they can best fulfill their mission."

—Stacey Sanders, Founder/Executive Director of Elevating Connections

"Very clear and thorough over what the foundation of any sustainable nonprofit needs to have. We found a few great nuggets that we had overlooked when we read the book."

—Carla M. Vaughn, Executive Director of Financial Literacy First

"An essential resource for nonprofit leaders desiring to focus on their mission, but they are too busy managing the day to day and putting out fires. Cindy brings advice that is practical, actionable, and grounded in her real-world experience. I know the sense of calm these resources and tactics can bring to any over-stressed Executive Director. A must-read for anyone leading a nonprofit."

—Mary Gaul, Owner Success Magnified

Contents

INTRODUCTION:

Ready to Build a More Successful Nonprofit?

THANK YOU FOR WHAT YOU DO. As a nonprofit professional, you make a difference in individual lives daily. This book is a resource for you as a nonprofit Executive Director, especially if you head a smaller nonprofit. When you build capacity and strengthen your organization, you can impact more people. When you implement systems and take care of yourself, you will find you have more confidence and endurance. As a bonus, you get to keep your sanity and have more fun.

You may be wondering who I am and why I am writing this book. I know your joy and frustration as Executive Director because I have over twenty-five years' experience in the nonprofit sector. I have had the privilege to serve as Executive Director/CEO for three organizations. I know what it takes to succeed.

When I got my first ED job, I was so excited. Being an Executive Director was one of my lifetime goals. I had just completed my master's degree as a single parent. I remember working three jobs, going to school full time, and raising a son. I kept thinking, *It's going to be worth it*. I still remember the interview process as if it were yesterday. I was the one selected to be the new Executive Director of Collin County Chapter of the American Red Cross.

In the first week on the job, I discovered we were not in compliance with the national organization. We had one year to get there, or our chapter would be disbanded. I did not want to fail at my first ED job. I was committed to succeeding just like you are. Thanks to the help and support of others, one by one I checked off the requirements. And before the deadline, we were back in compliance.

We went from being a one-county, noncompliant chapter with a budget of less than $300,000 to a four-county, compliant chapter with a budget of over $1 million. This led to my promotion to CEO for the American Red Cross of North Texas and serving as State Leader and Regional and National Trainer, helping to build stronger nonprofit leaders. I even had the privilege to serve as the dean and on the faculty for new Chapter Executive Orientation for the Southwestern Region of the American Red Cross.

When I moved back to Colorado, I was hired as Executive Director for a small, independent, thirty-year-old nonprofit that was struggling. Its future was in question. The situation was all too familiar. What would have happened if I did not have my background and prior experience to guide the organization to meet its challenges and ensure its success? There was no support or oversight to show me the way. Thankfully, I was able to strengthen and build capacity for future growth for that organization.

At one time I thought about returning to school to get my PhD, so I could support and impact new Executive Directors. As I did the research, I discovered the academic environment focused more on research and theory than actual implementation. I know from experience that you need real-world guidance, not theory. Instead of going back to school, I decided to write this book. I wanted to share tips, tools, and strategies to make your job easier with the most efficient and effective ways to get results for your agency.

This book is a blueprint to help you lead a well-run agency. The information will work for you whether you are a new Executive Director or have been an Executive Director for a while and are looking for ways to streamline and improve your organization.

This book will not cover all facets of running a successful nonprofit agency, rather it will share ways to simplify and streamline your organization. The goal is to create an infrastructure that will run with or without you. When you have systems in place to manage the day-to-day operations, it will allow you to focus on future development and strategic relationships.

You may be thinking, "I am doing okay. Our agency is providing services according to our mission."

Think about what it would look like to serve more people with less stress and have more time for yourself. With better systems and tracking, you can show your outcomes to funders more effectively. If you like this idea, please keep reading.

Do You Have a House of Straw – Or a House of Bricks?

Do you remember the story of *The Three Little Pigs*? Each pig had built their own house. One was built with straw, one with sticks, and one with bricks. This metaphor reflects many nonprofit organizations. Some are just struggling to get by – their "house of straw" can barely stand on its own. Meanwhile, others are well-built with solid foundations – their "house of bricks" is thriving, growing, and serving more people daily.

For the Three Little Pigs, life was good until the Big Bad Wolf came along. When tough times happen, and they will, is your organization prepared? One by one, we saw two of the little pigs' houses get destroyed. How many nonprofits do you know that have shut their doors during difficult times?

In the story, the pigs with the houses built of straw and sticks did not fare well when adversity struck. The house built of bricks could sustain the Big Bad Wolf, and life continued. In fact, the brick house owner provided shelter for the other two little pigs. Similarly, in the nonprofit sector agencies sometimes merge to be able to survive and thrive.

My goal is to help you ensure your organization is built like the house of bricks, so it can endure any hardship that comes your way. The "wolf" could come in many forms for a nonprofit, especially a smaller nonprofit. Perhaps the adversity would be similar to one of these situations:

- The organization is in jeopardy of losing its nonprofit status for noncompliance.
- A funder asks for detailed program outcomes that you do not have readily available.
- A key staff member or Board member leaves suddenly, and your agency does not have a contingency plan in place.
- You're feeling overwhelmed, with a lack of direction.

What could the "wolf" (adversity) be for your agency? Take a moment to think about that question. We'll come back to this story at the end of this book.

Steps to Build a Strong, Well-Run Nonprofit

Just as the pigs needed to construct a house to live in, you need to build an agency that can deliver the organization's mission to the people you serve. Let's think about what it takes to build a house. While you may never have thought about the steps involved, it is a straightforward process of moving from a design concept to the finished project.

Here is a basic overview of the steps involved in construction:
- The blueprint is the first step to determine what you want the results to look like or, in our case, how you want to carry out your mission.

- The next step is to hire a general contractor or, in our case, an Executive Director. The Board of Directors will maintain oversight of the project, while the Executive Director manages daily operations.
- Next, we will add the "rooms" or areas of responsibility, followed by the systems needed for operation.
- The "final inspection" is the last step of the construction process. In our case, this is the end-of-year review and audit.

This is a simplified way to look at the "construction" steps to build a well-run organization and without you, as the Executive Director, losing your sanity. Remember, we want to Simplify to Serve.

Each chapter follows this construction metaphor with real-world advice to create a solid, well-built agency that will survive adversity and deliver valuable services to your community well into the future. In addition, each chapter includes Growth Action Steps, which guide you to personally build a foundation to Simplify to Serve. The goal is to prompt you for needed actions with ideas you can implement to build the foundation for a strong, healthy organization.

While this book covers a lot of topics, it does not address every aspect of running a successful organization, like fundraising and program evaluation. The goal of this book is to help you put systems and processes in place to allow you more time to work on fundraising, program delivery, and other areas needing your attention. Think of this knowledge as the foundation for you to build a strong, sustainable organization.

To clarify terms, throughout the book the words *agency* and *organization* are interchangeable. The titles *Executive Director* and *Chief Executive Officer* (paid staff or volunteer) are interchangeable as well as *Board Chair* and *Board President* (volunteer). Staff can refer to paid or volunteer staff. The focus is on 501(c)(3) nonprofit organizations and volunteer-led groups like community service organizations.

Each time you review this book, you and the agency will be in a different place. It will take time and dedication to create a smooth-running organization. Utilizing these concepts to build a solid foundation, we will explore how to help you lead with more confidence and less stress while building a strong agency, so you can better serve and deliver your mission.

You may find it helpful to download the *Agency Assessment Checklist – How Are You Doing?* At my website, www.NonprofitSuccessNetwork. com, before you begin reading this book. It can help you identify areas that may need attention.

Now, let's begin the process.

CHAPTER 1:

The Initial "Design and Blueprint" Stages

WHAT DOES YOUR IDEAL NONPROFIT ORGANIZATION LOOK LIKE?
Who are you serving? Who is helping you carry out your mission? Keeping in compliance with state and federal requirements and having current information listed on GuideStar and Charity Navigator is like getting building permits and inspections for your organization. These activities need to be completed regularly and with attention to detail.

This section is about creating the blueprint for your ideal organization. The agency bylaws and mission statement are the compass for your organization. The mission statement will keep you focused and on track. Use the mission statement as a litmus test when you are discussing a new direction or adding new services.

Mission drift is a common problem when agencies are struggling and trying to survive. Mission drift can occur when a funding opportunity for a new program or direction is available, yet it is outside the scope of the mission. When you stay focused on the mission, you can thrive.

Staying focused on your mission helps you clearly see priorities and limit the drama. Imagine your life without drama. Drama does not just walk into your life. Either you create it, invite it, or associate with it. As the key leader for your organization, you have the responsibility to be sure everyone knows what to do and when to do it. When your agency has a clear mission and a written Plan of Action in place that is shared and referred to often, you will find it is more difficult for drama to find a way in the door. Remember, your goal is a well-run agency with less stress and more fun.

One of the best practices is to have a timeline or Annual Master Calendar with all dates recorded, so everyone is aware of what needs to happen and when. You can also establish sub-calendars, such as administrative, program, Board, and so forth.

Get Your House in Order: IRS Forms and Compliance

First things first – do you have your IRS 501(c)(3) tax-exempt letter? This letter is priceless. This letter gives you the authority to solicit funds as a charitable organization and reduce the sales tax you may pay. You may want to protect your original letter with a sheet protector. You and your staff will need this letter often. It may be helpful to have paper copies available, and place the electronic scanned file on the organization's shared drive.

Do you have a fire safe or a locked file cabinet to store important agency records? If not, I highly recommend purchasing a fire safe or locked file cabinet for the safety and security of key documents.

Is your nonprofit registered with your secretary of state? Be sure to check if your state requires multiple registrations. Some states require you to be listed as a business, a charity, and an authorized charity to solicit funds.

When I work with clients, this is one of the first questions I ask them: "Are you registered with the state?" Most of the time, they are registered but have not completed all the different required registrations.

As the key leader, it is your responsibility to be sure the organization stays in compliance with federal, state, and local regulations. The Annual Master Calendar can be helpful to ensure you get volunteer input and help as needed in time to meet the deadlines. It is important you share this information with the Board of Directors who have the ultimate fiduciary responsibility for the organization.

Getting inspections to show the work has been completed correctly is part of the construction process. In the nonprofit world, one way to show the organization's accomplishments is with a current GuideStar and Charity Navigator organizational listing.

Depending on the annual gross receipts, as a 501(c)(3) charitable organization you are required to file a Form 990 annually: Form 990-N (small agency with gross annual receipts of less than $50,000), Form 990-EZ (short form), and the full Form 990. Check the IRS website for current filing requirements.

At the time of printing, for agencies with a calendar fiscal year the due date for filing is May fifteenth or five months after the end of your fiscal year if you are required to file. It is important to file on time or file for an extension. Check with a CPA for more information.

While an accountant may complete the Form 990 itself, you have an opportunity to use the 990 to tell your story about the services you provide to the community and the impact you have on your clients. The 990 information is published on GuideStar and Charity Navigator. You can add supplemental information to Form 990. This is your chance to highlight your outcomes – the impact your nonprofit has on your clients.

Be sure to scan the completed, signed 990 tax return and save it on the organization's shared drive. Place the physical copy in your locked file cabinet for future reference. When applying for grants and other funding opportunities, you may be asked to submit a copy of your 990 tax returns.

Improve Your GuideStar and Charity Navigator Listings

Once you have spent the time and energy to maximize your exposure by describing your services and impact, now is the time to take it to the next level. Both GuideStar and Charity Navigator use the 990 as the basis for your organization's listing. GuideStar provides data on nonprofits, foundations, and grants. GuideStar provides this service free of charge to nonprofits, which can edit and update their listings. Having a robust listing is important, since this is where potential donors, volunteers, and staff check out your organization.

While GuideStar does not give you a rating system, it does provide you with a Seal of Transparency. With minimum effort, you can improve your listing from name and basic contact information to a Bronze, Silver, Gold, or Platinum level. Organizations can earn the Seal of Transparency based on the types of information they choose to share. You'll find free resources like the GuideStar Common Results Catalog and more detailed information on the Seal of Transparency.

During one of my courses, the Executive Director of Sickle Cell Reproductive Health Education Directive was just launching her organization and went from a basic listing to Gold Level of Transparency as a new agency.

With a good business plan and well-defined goals and objectives, you can present your agency well. The key is submitting the required documentation to GuideStar. GuideStar provides a place for nonprofits to showcase their programs and community impact. According to GuideStar, Seal of Transparency nonprofits saw an increase of 53 percent more in contributions than organizations that were less transparent. Plus, donor loyalty increased with transparency.

Charity Navigator offers full listings for organizations that have $1,000,000 in revenue for two consecutive years, at least $500,000 in public support/contributions, and seven years of Form 990 filings. It also offers an Encompass Rating System for smaller charities. This is an additional opportunity to show you are a well-run nonprofit organization.

The Charity Navigator Encompass Rating System for smaller charities is available to those who have 990 filings for three consecutive years (Forms 990-PF, 990-EZ, 990-N are not sufficient). Based on the information you provide Charity Navigator generates a rating using the Four Beacons of Organizational Effectiveness:

- Finance & Accountability
- Impact & Results
- Leadership & Adaptability
- Culture & Community

Check the Charity Navigator website for current requirements. Some Board policies requirements for this website include your organization's conflict of interest policy, document retention and destruction policy, and whistleblower policy. Every organization should have these policies in place.

Charity Navigator scores ratings from 0 to100, with a score of 75 or above indicating effectiveness and transparency. Those organizations earn a Give with Confidence designation that is displayed on Charity Navigator's website. This is one more way to show potential donors you are worthy of their financial support.

The free services GuideStar and Charity Navigator offer help ensure best practices for the nonprofit sector. While you currently may be a small organization, you want to protect your organization's assets, including your public image and reputation. While it may take some time in the first year to prepare and submit all the documentation, it is well worth the effort involved.

You will need to review the listing on these two websites annually to check for accuracy and updated requirements. An easy way to handle this task is to look at the Annual Master Calendar and the workload. Choose two light-workload months and add the task to update one website each month with the current information.

Join Other Organizations

Two additional places to consider listing your nonprofit organization are your state association of nonprofits (if one is available) and the local chamber of commerce. While these organizations usually require a membership fee, if you take advantage of training and networking opportunities your membership will easily pay for itself. Think of the membership fee as an investment in your agency.

By joining professional organizations, both you and the nonprofit can benefit from your involvement. Joining the local chamber of commerce can be an excellent way to make community connections while you benefit from the networking events and trainings the chamber offers. Also, take a moment to check if your state has an association of nonprofits. Membership can be an excellent investment. Plus, your membership may include discount pricing on services.

Be actively involved with your state association of nonprofits and your local chamber of commerce. Your presence will increase your personal knowledge through training and learning about community needs and resources. This involvement also increases the organization's exposure. You want to be top of mind, so when opportunity presents itself business and nonprofit leaders will immediately seek you and your organization.

When community organizations, such as the chamber of commerce and the state association of nonprofits list you as a member on their website, this is an added bonus. This type of exposure increases your credibility and visibility. Take time to ensure the membership rosters accurately list your agency description.

Maintaining your external presence and requirements can be over-whelming. This is where the Annual Master Calendar can be extremely helpful. Some dates are mandated, like tax returns and state registration. Once you have input the required dates, you can schedule each month to review one of the listings mentioned above. The key is reducing your workload and being consistent. You want to have a well-run nonprofit organization without losing your sanity. Remember, Simplify to Serve.

CONSIDER THESE GROWTH ACTION STEPS

KNOWLEDGE WITHOUT ACTION is incomplete. When you learn something, you need to take action to benefit from this new knowledge. The list below presents a variety of suggested action steps. As you read this chapter, you may have thought of other needed actions. Start where you are and expand as your time and scope permit. Think of this book as a reference source – each time you read it you and your agency will be in a different place, and you can take the needed steps for where you are at that time.

Choose one or more of the following to put into practice:

- Create an Annual Master Calendar for your agency.
- Put the dates for federal and state tax forms for your 501(c)(3) agency on your Annual Master Calendar.
- Review and update your GuideStar and/or Charity Navigator listing and put a note on the calendar to schedule the next update.
- Work on upgrading your GuideStar Seal of Transparency level to the next level.
- Join a membership organization (your state association of nonprofits, chamber of commerce, or a professional organization).
- Design your own action step.

MY GROWTH ACTION PLAN

ACTION	DUE BY	DONE

CHAPTER 2:

The Executive Director as "General Contractor"

WOULD YOU START A BUILDING PROJECT without first hiring a general contractor? Probably not. This individual oversees the entire project and communicates regularly with the different parties.

In the case of a nonprofit organization, this individual is usually the Executive Director or Chief Executive Officer. As you know, this individual is appointed by the Board of Directors and may be paid or a volunteer. This person manages the day-to-day operations and is responsible for implementing the organization's mission. Selecting the right general contractor is key to a successful building project. Likewise, selecting the right person to lead the nonprofit as Executive Director is key to the success of the agency.

A detailed job description is the basis for appointing or hiring an Executive Director. To write an accurate and complete job description, the Board of Directors will benefit from conducting an agency assessment and determining the strengths needed to accomplish the organizational goals at the present time.

Organizational goals will change over time. Sometimes, the nonprofit will need an individual with strong community relationship skills and fundraising experience. Other times, the organization will need someone with the ability to create a strong infrastructure with a robust volunteer component to carry out the mission. An objective assessment can help the organization identify the current top priority for the agency, especially when hiring the new Executive Director.

If you are the new Executive Director, you will want to do your own agency assessment to determine which areas need your immediate attention. Building relationships with your Board of Directors is always a first step. It may be beneficial to schedule individual meetings with Board members to learn about them and understand their expectations and motivations.

Another piece to consider is what future funding looks like for the agency. While funding may look good for today, be sure to look forward to future years when grants expire, investments mature, and so forth. Be sure you clearly understand when you will need to adjust to accommodate the financial changes.

When I did my first agency assessment, I learned that if we did not change our method of operation we would not have the needed funding in five years. Several of our bonds were maturing at a high rate of return, while the current environment did not offer anything close to our return rate. We immediately created a financial development strategy, allowing us to close the gap at a critical point. Without this knowledge, those bonds would have expired, and we would have been in dire straits. Forecasting and planning ahead can save you and the agency stress and create an environment of stability and confidence.

Practical Tips to Become a Better Leader

The Board of Directors has placed their trust in you to manage the nonprofit organization as their Executive Director. As the "general contractor" for the organization, your leadership abilities will be critical. Leadership is the art of motivating groups of people to act toward a common goal.

As you may have already discovered, you will be interacting with a variety of people in many diverse settings. Your relationships with them will vary as well. Your ability to adapt will be critical to your personal success as well as to your organization. It is helpful to know your own leadership style and how you react in different situations. Sometimes you will lead; sometimes you will follow. Learn to know which is needed given the situation.

The better you know yourself, the better you will be able to lead your agency. A variety of personality and leadership assessment tools are available. Many are offered at no cost. It can be beneficial to study and learn at least one assessment tool that you can immediately utilize in your daily operations. When you learn to utilize an assessment tool you can share the knowledge with others, which will strengthen your own knowledge and understanding.

Here are just a few examples of how a personality assessment can make a difference in facilitating your progress and success as a leader.

The DISC assessment is common in for-profit and nonprofit organizations. The DISC assessment measures four main personality styles: Dominance, Influence, Steadiness, and Conscientiousness. Tony Robbins offers a free DISC assessment on his website if you have never taken it and want to see your profile. Understanding your staff members' DISC profile can help you better manage and encourage your team members. It can help you balance skill sets when you hire new employees. Your goal is a well-rounded team with a variety of experiences and skills.

Myers-Briggs Type Indicator (MBTI) is another common personality assessment. The MBTI uses sixteen personality types to measure a combination of these preferences: extroversion or introversion, sensing or intuition, feeling or thinking, judging or perceiving. This assessment will help you understand yourself and others better.

It can offer insight into the behavior of your Board members, volunteers, and staff. For example, a person can demonstrate extroverted skills when their preference is introverted. This would be important to know when you are showing your appreciation for their involvement. The extrovert loves a big celebration, especially in their honor, while an introvert may prefer a more low-key event. Remember, each person is an individual. As you continue to establish better relationships, you will continue to learn about all the individuals on your team and their preferences.

My personal favorite is the Color Code Personality Assessment by Taylor Hartman, PhD. This assessment divides personality styles into four colors: red, blue, white, and yellow. The Color Code addresses the internal motivation – driving core motives. This can be extremely helpful since nonprofits tend to work with many volunteers. Knowing and focusing on volunteers' motivation will increase their satisfaction and loyalty to you and the organization.

By including this assessment in the Board training when I was an Executive Director, we were able to establish a common language and have tools to help redirect discussions if they became too intense. By using a statement like, "Your red [behavior] is coming out; we need a little more blue," the group could understand that they needed to show more compassion to the other members. This simple redirect would lighten the mood, and the conversation could continue in a respectful manner. This was probably not Dr. Hartman's intention, yet it worked to our benefit.

The more you understand human nature and the behavior of others, the better you will be able to manage and build your organization. It begins with knowing yourself first. You are the one who must adapt if you want to survive and thrive as an Executive Director and be a true leader for your organization. Remember, you are in partnership with the Board of Directors.

Each year, you may have a different Board Chair and that person's style will be different. One year you may have Chair A who is action orientated, with limited time available for the organization. You will need to have discussion materials together with an agenda each time you meet to maximize the limited time allotted to you. The following year you may have Board Chair B who is all about building relationships. This individual may want to get to know you and share about themselves and their family. Each meeting, you may spend a few minutes sharing and reconnecting before you get down to business.

Imagine if you approached Chair A with chitchat about the family before addressing the matter at hand or if you started your conversation with Chair B about the task before reconnecting on a personal level first. This may seem minor, yet knowing personal styles can solidify and propel your relationships to a new level when you understand individuals and their needs and motivations.

Reading and understanding people are critical skills when you are working with volunteers and, especially, the Board of Directors. Since volunteers receive no paychecks, you must motivate and recognize them in a way that is comfortable and desirable for them. Some people love the spotlight, while others would be nervous in the spotlight. Learn about your people and invest in those relationships. Your return will be tremendous. You can't do the job alone; you need their help. A simple notecard of appreciation can go a long way to enhance relationships and stay connected.

As a key leader in your organization, it's important to develop good working relationships with the current Board members. Simultaneously, you can be building the Board of your dreams. While the original Board of Directors hired you, remember that Board terms may be term limited according to your nonprofit's bylaws. One of your first steps will be to conduct an assessment of Board members' occupations, skills and talents, and community connections. Using a Board Grid or a spreadsheet can give you a snapshot of the demographics and expertise you have and highlight the areas needing improvement.

The skills and expertise needed will vary based on your organization.

All nonprofit agencies need access to individuals with a strong financial and accounting background, legal and human resources knowledge, and marketing and fundraising abilities. A Board that has diverse experience, ethnicity, and culture will be stronger, allowing you to reach more people. The Board Grid is a simple tool that helps you monitor and demonstrate your commitment to diversity, equity, and inclusion (DEI).

Work with your Nominating Committee to identify potential Board candidates and the leadership skills your nonprofit needs. Within three to five years the Board of your dreams is possible. You and the Board are in partnership, and you want to build a strong team to carry out the mission of the organization.

Once you have your target list of ideal Board members, you can start the search process. It is a happy day when you identify an interested individual as a potential board candidate. For example, let's say you have a conversation with a colleague you met through the local chamber of commerce. She is a Black, female accountant who expressed an interest in your agency's mission. Depending on the needs of the organization, you may be able to improve in three areas by recruiting one volunteer. When you have your ideal list of candidates clearly defined, it is easier to find those potential volunteer candidates for your Board.

Leadership Tips That May Surprise You

As noted above, the more you understand human nature and the behavior of others, the better you will be able to manage and build your organization. Similarly, as the agency's leader, you must understand your own nature and needs. You must take care of yourself.

You may be a parent as well as an Executive Director. When you travel in an airplane, the flight attendant tells you to put your oxygen mask on first before you put the mask on your children. The same is true in the agency – you must take care of yourself first and then think about the organization and the people involved.

Setting healthy boundaries is critical. You will need to keep balance in your life. When you become unbalanced it creates stress, which can lead to illness. Many times, the health status of the Executive Director will reflect the health status of the organization. You want to be healthy personally, so you can lead a healthy organization that is strong and sustainable.

Have you ever thought about what your life would look like in a snapshot? Imagine viewing your life as a wheel – would your life be well-rounded? Using a life-balance assessment tool, you can check to see if your life is in balance. You may want to check out the Wheel of Life or the Wellness Inventory. Both tools provide you with a visual picture of your life in eight to twelve areas, depending on the assessment tool. While your life will never be perfectly well rounded, it is helpful to recognize the areas you may be avoiding or neglecting.

The Wellness Inventory will give you a visual sense of what your life looks like utilizing twelve dimensions and will send you email reminders to help you stay on track. For example, spending the vast majority of your time at work – including evenings and weekends – does not lead to a well-rounded, healthy lifestyle. Email reminders can help you create boundaries, so you have the time and energy to address other important facets of your life. If you think this tool could help you, please contact me to learn more. I am a Wellness Inventory Certified Coach and would be happy to provide details.

One simple way to create boundaries for yourself is by establishing and clearly communicating the hours you are available. When Executive Directors first start out, they want to be accessible. They say, "Call me anytime; I'm always available." While that will work for a while, it will not work long term if you want to avoid burnout. You have a right to a life and some privacy. Remember, you want to lead a well-run nonprofit without losing your sanity!

You must have time to recharge and address the other areas of your life beyond the scope of your role as Executive Director. What do you need to maintain a healthy lifestyle? Maybe it is: "I don't take calls after 7:00 p.m. or on weekends unless it's an emergency." Sure, there will be exceptions depending on your agency's services. Perhaps you need to be on call during natural disasters or while your organization's summer camp is running. The key is to define what you need personally and still be of service to the agency.

Another simple way to create time and space for yourself is to establish guidelines. While maintaining an open-door policy can build trust and open communication, you still need to establish a boundary. If the door is closed, you are unavailable at this time unless it's an emergency. Creating a quiet environment for planning or budgeting can be extremely helpful when you don't have interruptions.

Also, learn to say "no" when appropriate. You can ask yourself the question, "If I say yes to this request, what am I saying no to?" This is beneficial if you are a people-pleaser and don't want to hurt someone's feelings. When you overcommit, you will inevitably let someone down – and it is usually yourself. You need to keep commitments to yourself just as you do for other people. Never apologize for self-care. When you take care of yourself, you will show up ready and able to serve and lead the agency.

When demands are high, sometimes it is difficult to schedule self-care. Be proactive and schedule an R&R Meeting on your calendar. (Think of it as a light at the end of the tunnel.) When someone looks at your shared calendar, they will see that you are booked and unavailable at this time. You might be asking, "What is an R&R Meeting?" It stands for *rest and relaxation*, essentially, a meeting with yourself. Similar to a mental health day, an hour-long (or day-long) R&R Meeting helps you keep your sanity and return to your projects refreshed, recharged, and ready to go.

Author Stephen Covey talks about keeping your saw sharpened in *The 7 Habits of Highly Effective People*. One way to sharpen your saw – your skills – is to be involved in personal and professional development. You need both to continue to grow and learn, ultimately making you a better person and leader.

If you are seeking a formal education, you may want to consider a degree or certification program specializing in nonprofit management. The Nonprofit Leadership Alliance began training nonprofit professionals in 1948 as American Humanics. Today it provides leadership training and resources for individuals to become a Certified Nonprofit Professional (CNP). The key is to continue to learn and develop your skill set.

We talked about joining the local chamber of commerce and your state association of nonprofits, and you may want to consider joining other organizations to help further your skills and professional development. If your nonprofit has a national association related to your target clients, consider joining to stay current on best practices and trends for your specific population. Attending a national conference is an excellent opportunity to expand your network and program ideas.

Many national organizations have a local chapter you can also join. The Association of Fundraising Professionals is a great example where you can build relationships, gain knowledge through training, and learn best practices.

Being part of a community service organization, such as Rotary International or Lions Club International, can help you give back to the community in other ways than just through your agency's services. By working in partnership with other organizations, it will increase community awareness about your agency.

Seventy percent of nonprofit professionals are women. If you are a woman, you may want to consider joining a women's professional business organization as well. Women experience different challenges and obstacles, and it can be helpful to have a network of other professional women to support you in your career.

The organizations mentioned above all have a volunteer component, which allows you to become involved in leadership capacities. This can be a great benefit to expand your knowledge and skills in areas that may or may not be part of your current position. Your involvement can also expose you to potential career opportunities. An important part of taking care of yourself is taking care of your career. We will talk more about this in a later chapter.

A growing area of support for professionals is the benefit of coaching and mastermind groups. Coaching is different from counseling or therapy. Counseling and therapy sessions usually focus on the past and on emotional issues; they may even deal with mental illness. Coaching typically focuses on the future and actions needed for change. In coaching, the foundational philosophy is that you have everything you need inside of you, you are healthy and whole, and you are complete just as you are. The coaching experience is achieved as the coach guides the client through exploring different options and behaviors and noticing how the results can change.

Coaching can be individual or in a group setting. This is an opportunity for you to share your challenges and struggles in a confidential setting where you get a different perspective and see how to move forward to achieve success. Coaching can also serve as a form of accountability. When you tell someone verbally you are going to do something, you experience a stronger commitment to make it actually happen.

Author Napoleon Hill in his book, *Think and Grow Rich*, talks about the advantages of a mastermind group. Being part of a peer advisory board or a mastermind group is extremely advantageous to expand your thinking. This group can provide feedback and input on your current projects. A sense of collaboration and synergy develops among group members, which expands possibilities.

When you are considering joining a group, you will want to clarify if it is for business professionals or exclusively for nonprofit Executive

Directors. Each type of group offers advantages and drawbacks. The key is to be sure you feel comfortable and are willing to fully engage to maximize your involvement in the mastermind experience. The other members will benefit from your participation just as you will profit from their involvement.

These groups usually commit to a six-to-twelve-month period to allow time for the group to develop trust and understanding of each other. Some groups have been together for years, and they have helped each other grow and expand their organizations.

Your wellbeing is the most important asset you have. Treat your life like a precious gift that has been given to you. It is your responsibility to take care of it. While you hold the position as Executive Director and leader of your organization, remember this is just one part of your life. Please don't neglect the other aspects of your life.

As Executive Director, many times you will feel like the Lone Ranger, but you can't do it alone. Building a highly capable, highly motivated team is essential to enable your organization to achieve its mission. Your ability to inspire and energize others will help to simplify the organization and your personal life.

CONSIDER THESE GROWTH ACTION STEPS

Here are some possible actions to grow your agency:

- Conduct an agency assessment – areas include Board development and financial development.
- Use a personality or leadership assessment tool to learn and understand your own leadership style.
- Study and teach a personality or leadership assessment tool to your organization.
- Create a Board Grid, and then work with the Nominating Committee to develop an ideal list for potential Board members.
- Reflect on your own needs for self-care.
- Design your own action step.

MY GROWTH ACTION PLAN

ACTION	DUE BY	DONE

CHAPTER 3:

Working Effectively with Your Board of Directors

LET'S TAKE A CLOSER LOOK at the Board of Directors. How do the Board members know what to do and when to do it? A professional, proactive Board of Directors is key to the success of your organization. The Board determines the future vision for the organization, and the Executive Director or Chief Executive Officer makes that vision a reality.

As the Executive, you are in charge of executing the policies, programs, and initiatives set by the Board of Directors. Plus, you must ensure the Board's success by making sure they have the information and tools they need to effectively set the direction for the organization in accordance with the mission.

The relationship between the Executive Director and the Board of Directors, especially the Board Chair, can be the most rewarding or the most challenging relationship you will encounter in your career. Each year, you may have a new Board Chair and that person's management style will be different from the previous person's style. Remember, it is your responsibility to adjust to their styles and preferences. You are working at the pleasure of the Board. You have your responsibilities, and the Board has its responsibilities.

To help clarify the responsibilities of the Board of Directors and the Executive Director, let's look at the difference between governance and management.

Here is a brief overview of the Board of Directors' fiduciary responsibilities. Every Board member has three duties:

- Duty of Care – Having the same care and concern as any prudent and ordinary person.
- Duty of Loyalty – Putting the nonprofit interest ahead of your own (avoiding conflict of interest).
- Duty of Obedience – Ensuring the nonprofit abides by the law.

Keep it simple. Remember CLOD = Care, Loyalty, Obedience, Duties.

Be sure to cover this information in Board training and include it in the *Board Manual* for easy reference. If you are not familiar with these responsibilities, you can readily find many resources online that discuss the Board of Directors' fiduciary responsibilities. For example, this article by Nick Price on the BoardEffect website, "The Fiduciary Responsibilities of a Nonprofit Board of Directors," is informative and easy to read.

Understanding the Board of Directors' fiduciary responsibilities is an excellent place to start the conversation about governance and management. The Board is responsible for the governance of the organization. The Board sets the policies and strategic direction for the organization, while the Executive Director implements those policies and strategies. While the areas of responsibility are clearly defined, it is truly a partnership with the agency's mission foremost in mind.

As a side note, directors and officers insurance is a good investment and worth exploring for your organization. Directors and Officers (D&O) liability insurance is intended to protect individuals from personal losses if they are sued as a result of serving as a director or officer of a nonprofit. It can also cover the legal fees and other costs the organization may incur as a result of such a suit.

It is important to remember that you, as the Executive Director, have been hired by the Board of Directors, and you are an employee of the organization. In some cases, this may be a volunteer position, yet the supervisory relationship remains the same as for a paid employee. As a nonprofit Executive Director, you are in a unique situation: while answering to the Board as an employee, you also have the responsibility to keep Board members on task for their responsibilities. It is truly a partnership if you are going to lead a well-run, successful organization.

That is why creating a job description listing all Board responsibilities, goals, and tasks is so crucial. This detailed document assures complete transparency. Plus, it supports accountability – being sure every job gets done, so everyone is carrying out the agency's mission according to the Strategic Plan, which is based on the mission.

You will also want to have a Letter of Commitment for all Board members – essentially the job requirements for that year. This document spells out the expectations for the Board members' and their responsibilities. You may want to include details regarding the minimum required attendance at Board and committee meetings, whether each Board member is expected to give or raise a specific amount in financial support, and if you expect these individuals to participate in program activities and fundraising events. This Letter of Commitment will be specific to your organization and the organizational goals for that year.

Keep in mind that the organization's bylaws may include some requirements for Board members. The bylaws are the rules that govern the nonprofit organization. It is important to follow the bylaws that the Board of Directors has adopted. Periodically, you will want to review your bylaws to see if they need to be amended to reflect your current operation or if you need to adjust any procedures to ensure they adhere to the bylaws. Think of the bylaws as a way of staying in compliance with the organization and your agency's mission.

The organization's bylaws may require or allow for the formation of an Executive Committee. This Board committee usually consists of the officers of the organization. Many times, this committee may have the authority to act for the organization when the full Board is not available with the understanding that the committee reports the action to the full Board, and it is captured in the Board minutes.

When you review the bylaws, this is a perfect time to start the Annual Master Calendar. If the bylaws list specific dates when certain events must occur, be sure to list them on this calendar. Examples include the date for the Annual Meeting and the process and timing for election of Board members and officers. Placing these events on a calendar will give you a visual representation of the year and workload. It can be helpful to have an Annual Master Calendar for the organization and a separate yearly Board Calendar with dates and events for Board attendance.

Your *Board Manual* Is an Important Communication Tool

One of the best tools to educate and inform Board members is a complete *Board Manual*. The manual will help them stay organized throughout the year and during their Board term. This manual can be a physical notebook or available online. It is the one place Board members can go to get answers to their questions. In addition, it reinforces their commitment and fiduciary responsibility to the organization.

Documents you might want to add to the *Board Manual* include:

- Welcome section
  - Welcome letter from the Board Chair and Executive Director
  - Signed Letter of Commitment
  - Board job description
  - Board leadership – officers and committee chairs

- Agency information
  - Agency fact sheet
  - Board roster – contact information
  - Calendar of events
  - Organizational chart – staff and volunteer

- History
  - Mission and Vision statements
  - Story of the agency's founding
  - Bylaws
  - Chart of Approval document
  - Board Policies and Procedures
  - Board action item format

- Goals
  - Annual goals
  - Strategic Plan

- Budget
  - Annual budget
  - Monthly financials

- Board meetings
  - Future agendas and minutes of past Board meetings

You may want to include additional items that are relevant to your organization, especially policies and procedures regarding the Board's fiduciary responsibilities. As an example, here's a commonly overlooked policy and procedure: Did you know the Board must record in its minutes all details regarding the agency's bank account as well as the authorized check signers? (The check signers may change when officers change, which requires additional Board action.) Further, the Board may want to establish policies to open credit card accounts and approve/accept all loans and grants. Without exception, all such items must be recorded in the Board minutes. This adds a level of transparency and protects the agency from abuse, ensuring no one can open and use accounts without Board approval. This action also helps to protect you as the Executive Director.

The National Council of Nonprofits offers excellent suggestions for Board orientation on its website. It may provide you with additional information to add to the *Board Manual*.

XYZ ORGANIZATION
APPROVAL LEVELS

Action	Department Director	Executive Director	Board Chair	Committee Recommendation	Committee Approval	Executive Committee	Full Board	Membership*	National*
Approve annual budget				X		X	X		
Appoint BD Committee Chairs			X			X	X		
Appoint BD Committee Members						X	X		
Appoint replacement BD members				X		X	X		
Approve annual audit report				X		X	X		X
Bank resolutions/signature authorizations							X		
Delegates to National Convention				X		X	X		
Designate Unrestricted Donation				X		X	X		
Elect new members to the board				X		X	X	X	
Elect BD Officers				X			X		
Endorse position papers on agency behalf				X		X	X		
Engage Auditor				X			X		
Hire Executive Director				X			X		X
Evaluate Executive Director						X	X		
Initiate new fundraising efforts				X		X	X		
Nominate individuals to National Board & Committees*				X		X	X		X
Paid & volunteer personnel policies				X		X	X		
Paid & volunteer personnel grievance resolutions					X				
Purchase under $1,000 budget item	X								
Purchase over $1,000 budget item		X							
Purchase unbudgeted item < $500		X							
Purchase unbudgeted item > $500 < $2,500						X	X		
Purchase over $2,500 (requires 3 competitive bids)				X		X	X		
Revisions to Board procedures				X		X	X		
Signature on contracts/grants/national docs			X			X	X		
Strategic/long-range plans				X		X	X		

Approved: (Date of Board Meeting)

* These items depend on organization and bylaws

This is an example of how an organization could structure its policies and procedures.

© Cynthia A "Cindy" Walters, MSSW, CNP

Useful Tool #1: The Chart of Approval

Two tools listed above – the Chart of Approval and the Board action item format – can help you streamline and clarify the approval process for your organization. The Chart of Approval is a quick reference of the policies and procedures the Board of Directors has established and adopted. If you already have policies in place, a spreadsheet layout gives you a summary on one page. For example, do you have guidelines or requirements for making purchases and who is authorized to make the purchase? Review the sample Chart of Approval and use this as a template for your nonprofit. While it may take some time to create a customized Chart of Approval for your agency, it is worth the investment to save time in the future and avoid misunderstandings.

Depending on the organization's bylaws, several items related to approving expenditures may already be defined. I encourage you to include them in the chart as well. The goal is to have a one-page, quick reference to make decisions while complying with your bylaws and policies.

In the sample chart, the top line includes the different individuals or groups involved in the action and decision making. The first column refers to the different action items. Notice that multiple people or groups may be involved. You can modify this chart to meet the needs of your organization. Generally, it will move from left to right in order of approval or action.

The sample Chart of Approval shows possible items to include. The key is to make it work for you and the Board of Directors. If you have staff, it can also help them understand the scope of decision making and their authority. For example, your team needs a replacement item to ensure your agency can continue to deliver services. Here are some questions to consider:

- Is it a budgeted item?
- How much does it cost?
- Does it cost over $2,500?

Using those questions, you can determine who ought to make the purchase. A budgeted item already has Board approval when the Board approves the annual budget. If the item is outside the scope of the approved budget, the cost will determine if the Executive Director can make the purchase or if it will require Board involvement. If the item is over $2,500, in this example your agency must obtain three competitive bids, and the expenditure requires committee recommendation and Board approval.

While this may seem like extra work, remember the Board has the fiduciary responsibility for the organization. As the Executive Director, you need to provide them with the necessary information to make an informed decision while complying with the bylaws. It also protects you as the Executive Director when you follow the established guidelines and policies.

It is important that the current, complete Chart of Approval includes the date of review or approval by the Board of Directors. This is part of the Board minutes and an organizational reference that will guide the agency to be sure it stays in compliance with its own policies and procedures.

Useful Tool #2: Board Action Item Format

One way to be respectful of Board members' time is to utilize the Board action item format. This will streamline the decision-making process and ensure all decisions have been thoroughly deliberated prior to the Board meeting. The Chart of Approval has a column titled Committee Recommendation – that is when you utilize the Board action item format.

While the details may appear self-explanatory, let's look at each detail independently. The components are similar to a memo. First, let's look at an easy way to organize your action items – use the last two digits of the fiscal year along with the next number in the sequence of action items the Board has addressed that year. Let's use the date August 31, 2022, as an example, and this is the sixth item coming before the Board this fiscal year. Let's say the agency operates a fiscal year ending June 30, 2023, so the year number would be 23 instead of 22. In this example, the proposed action item would be Board Action Item #23-06.

Take a look at the blank Board action item format. The "To" refers to who will be receiving this action item. While this is usually the Board of Directors, it can also be used for a committee if that is the first step for approval.

The "From" indicates the sponsor of this request. It may be an individual, the Executive Director, and/or a committee.

The "Date" is the date the action item is presented to the Board of Directors for approval. This facilitates tying it to Board minutes. If the Board revises or amends the action item, you would list the new date that the Board reviews it. While the original action item is maintained, you would change the title to "Amended Action Item #original number."

The "Re" is like the subject line in an email – a short explanation of the topic.

Action Item # YR-00

To: Board of Directors

From: ? Committee

Date: Board Meeting Date

Re:

1. Background

2. Proposed Action

3. Recommendation

4. Fiscal Impact

5. Impact on Service Delivery

Next, five parts provide an overview of the request:

1. Background – This describes the background that created the need for this change or action. It needs to be short and concise yet clear, so anyone reading it will understand the situation. This is achieved by having a thorough discussion at the committee level.
2. Proposed Action – This is the narrative about the proposed action, giving a brief overview of the solution.
3. Recommendation – Here you include the statement: "The (sponsor) Committee recommends adoption of Board Action Item #23-06 effective immediately (or the date it will become effective)."
4. Fiscal Impact – Here you detail the cost and financial effects. Points to consider include one-time or recurring costs, monthly or annual fees, a set amount or not to exceed request, and so forth. If this proposed action would result in lost revenue, it is stated here with an explanation. Sometimes, the action item has no fiscal impact, and you simply state this on the form.
5. Impact on Service Delivery – With the mission statement in mind, you want to describe the impact on clients and on the programs and services you offer. Results to consider are whether this action will help you provide better services, whether you will be able to better track your efforts to outcomes, whether this could reduce or eliminate services, and so forth. Usually, significant action items will impact service delivery.

To: Board of Directors

From: Your Name, Executive Director, and the Executive Committee

Date: September 21, 2022

Re: Paid Staff Leave during last week of December

1. Background

Since March 2022, the staff has taken a reduction in hours which resulted in a 10% reduction in pay for them individually. The week between Christmas and New Year's many offices close and traditionally very few if any clients have been seen during this time.

2. Proposed Action

It is recommended to close the office between Christmas and New Year's annually and provide the staff with paid time off during this time. If approved, this will be incorporated into the future Personnel Policies.

3. Recommendation

The Executive Committee recommends adoption of Action Item # 23-06 effective immediately.

4. Fiscal Impact

There will be no additional cost as (Your Agency) will be paying the staff if they work this week anyway. This year, the cost savings from the reduction in hours will more than cover the cost.

5. Impact on Service Delivery

There will be minimal, if any, impact on the clients. Individuals and companies are not usually interviewing and seeking employees this time of year.

Now let's look at a real-world example. Review the completed form – notice the agency used this format to provide brief, relevant information to the Board of Directors, so they can quickly review the key points and make an informed decision.

When you use this format to create a thorough discussion at the committee level, it will reduce the number of action items going to the full Board of Directors that are not worthy of consideration. I have found this to be an effective tool to streamline Board meetings. Be sure to include this form in the packet Board members receive a week in advance of the Board meeting. Board members are encouraged to contact the committee members if they have questions about the proposed action.

Not all action items will receive Board approval. However, utilizing this method will simplify Board meetings and eliminate digression from the matter at hand.

Build a Better Board: Orientation, Retreat, and Committees

Keep in mind that Board members are volunteers. Ongoing trainings and recognition are essential to retain your volunteers and keep them engaged and highly productive. Board orientation is the first step to onboard new Board members. It can be valuable if all Board members attend to build a stronger team for the organization. It can serve as a reminder to existing members of their responsibilities as a Board member. One way to help make that happen is to ask current Board members to carry out part of the event. Be sure to include the date for orientation and other Board meetings and trainings on the yearly Board Calendar.

Board retreats can be perfect for team building. An informal setting allows for friendships to develop while working together for a common goal. A strategic planning retreat can set the future direction for the organization. It can be helpful to secure an outside facilitator for your Board retreat to ensure you, as the Executive Director, can be fully engaged.

It is important to determine the desired outcome of the Board retreat before you begin planning. The more advanced notice you can give people, the better the attendance. This is where a separate yearly Board Calendar can be an asset.

During the year, a portion of the work may be done through the Board of Directors' committees. Each committee is led by a chair. The committee job description gives the scope and responsibilities for that committee. If the committees schedule regular meetings, place the dates on the yearly Board Calendar. Ideally, each committee would also have an Annual Plan of Action that aligns with the Strategic Plan.

The bylaws will determine specifics on the Annual Meeting and the election of Board members and officers. Once you add the Annual Meeting to the calendar, the process begins again with Board orientation for new Board members. And, once you establish the yearly Board Calendar, you will find the year will flow smoothly from year to year by just changing the dates for the current year. This simple action can save you time and energy. Remember, Simplify to Serve.

CONSIDER THESE GROWTH ACTION STEPS

Here are possible actions to grow your agency:

- Create and distribute the yearly Board Calendar.
- Create or update the *Board Manual* annually.
- Hold a Board orientation to train new Board members.
- Explore the idea of a Board retreat.
- Establish ways to recognize Board members.
- Develop a Chart of Approval for the organization.
- Use the Board action item format to streamline Board meetings.
- Design your own action step.

MY GROWTH ACTION PLAN

ACTION	DUE BY	DONE

CHAPTER 4:

Building Out the "Rooms" – Areas of Responsibility

AS THE EXECUTIVE DIRECTOR, you have the overall vision of the organization with an in-depth understanding of all the different components. You will know what actions are being taken by each staff member or volunteer as reflected in the written Plan of Action. Keeping with our construction metaphor, as the "general contractor" you have an overarching view of the many "rooms" or areas of responsibility.

The agency organizational chart can give you a visual of the structure of how your agency addresses the various areas. As the agency grows and expands, you might ultimately have separate Board and staff organizational charts to reflect the areas of responsibility. The organizational chart is your at-a-glance view of the human resource operation of your agency. (See the Sample Organizational Chart.)

Sample Organizational Chart

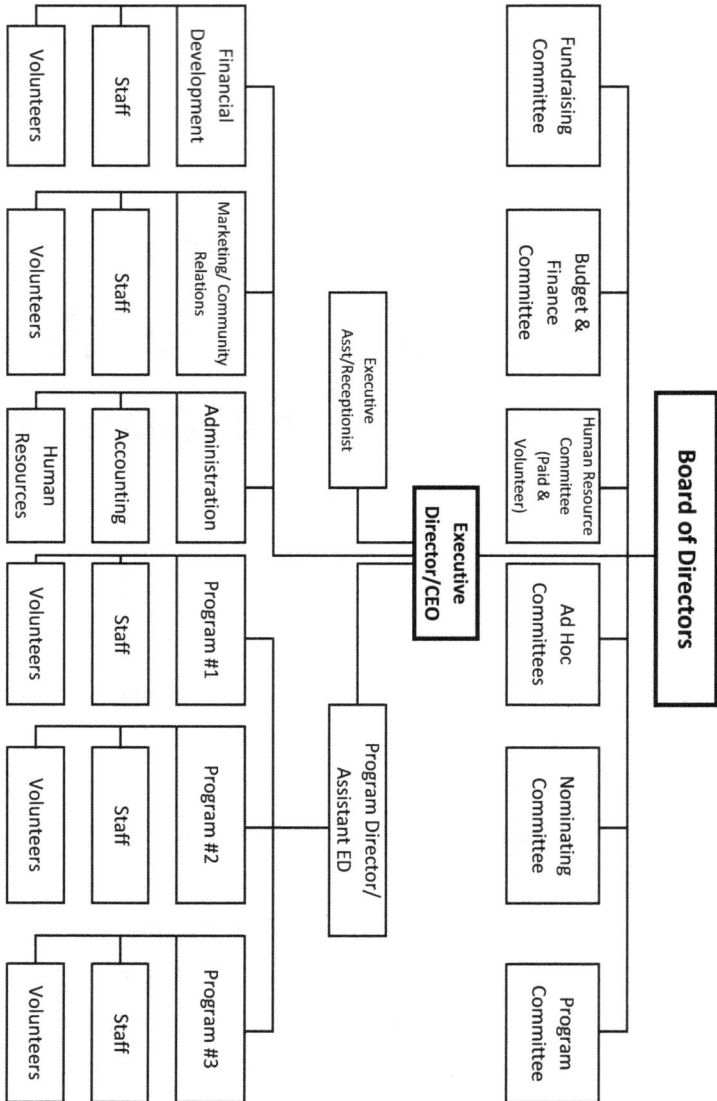

This is an example of a nonprofit organizational chart and will vary based on the bylaws and services of the organization.

Board of Directors

- Fundraising Committee
- Budget & Finance Committee
- Human Resource Committee (Paid & Volunteer)
- Ad Hoc Committees
- Nominating Committee
- Program Committee

Executive Director/CEO

- Executive Asst/Receptionist

- Financial Development
  - Staff
  - Volunteers
- Marketing/Community Relations
  - Staff
  - Volunteers
- Administration
  - Accounting
  - Human Resources

- Program Director/ Assistant ED
  - Program #1
    - Staff
    - Volunteers
  - Program #2
    - Staff
    - Volunteers
  - Program #3
    - Staff
    - Volunteers

It is important to consider several areas of responsibility, and organizations may choose how they want to address the different areas. When you conduct the strategic planning and design the committee structure, you will want to keep the various areas in mind. The most common areas may include Board fundamentals, community relations (including social media), fiduciary and fiscal responsibilities, financial development, human resources, programs and services, strategic planning, and technology. You can find a plethora of resources online for each of those areas.

For our purposes, we will talk about practices and processes to make your job easier and help to strengthen the organization. In each organization, the leaders need to decide what will work best for their organization. The agency bylaws will play a part in how you structure the agency.

When the volunteer structure and staff structure align, it is easier to maintain continuity of flow. Remember the Board is setting the direction, and the Executive Director is responsible for implementation, which means staff members and program volunteers are the responsibility of the Executive Director. It is worth noting this during Board training. Remind Board members that if they have a request of staff it comes through you as the Executive Director. Without this consistency, it can create conflict if staff members are receiving direction from multiple sources.

The Executive Director is ultimately responsible for all (paid or volunteer) staff actions. The Board of Directors can address issues with the Executive Director. Remember, you and the Board are in partnership to carry out the mission of the organization. Think of it as "us" rather than "we and they."

When the organization has paid staff, only the Executive Director reports to the Board. All staff members and program volunteers report to the Executive Director. It is important to maintain the chain of command. Otherwise, staff members can get confused when a Board member tells them one thing and the Executive Director gives them a different instruction. Keep in mind that while the Board is responsible for the vision, the Executive Director is responsible for implementation. This is where working in partnership will help to eliminate this potential challenge of conflicting instruction.

On occasion, Board members will also be program volunteers, creating a dual relationship. This can be challenging if you have not laid the proper foundation at Board orientation. When this occurs, it is important for Board members to remember which capacity they are serving in at that time. When Board members are serving in the Board capacity, the Executive Director is working for the Board. When Board members are serving as program volunteers, the Executive is the supervisor.

It is worth having a conversation with each individual in this situation at the beginning of a program event when someone is serving in both roles concurrently. Plus, it is helpful to have this conversation with the Board Chair, so they understand this unique situation and can support you, should you need backup support in the future.

Staff (paid or volunteer) are individuals assigned to a position or task. You will need to build a team of dedicated individuals. Investing the time to select the right person for the right job will pay off in the long run. When you create an environment of trust and open communication, people will stay longer, which reduces turnover and increases loyalty to you and the organization. Ask yourself: "Would I do the task that I am asking my staff to do?" If not, consider how you can make the job or assignment more desirable. Your ability to read and understand people will aid you in knowing what motivates people and how to tap into their passion.

Staff Development

The organizational chart represents a picture of how the entire team will carry out the mission. Let's look at how to build and engage a team to carry out the service delivery. We talked about the importance of Board orientation for the Board of Directors – the same is true for paid or volunteer staff.

Staff development includes onboarding orientation, ongoing training, and recognition. For orientation, you may want to develop an overview of the agency and its history that is applicable to everyone. You can then add position-specific training and education. This would include a written job description and Annual Plan of Action, so everyone knows what is expected of them. (We'll take a closer look at the Annual Plan of Action later in this chapter.)

A job description can be simple or complex. Templates are readily available online. Job descriptions just need to include:

- Job title (add department if applicable)
- Report to (supervisor's title)
- Job summary (one-sentence description of the job)
- Supervisory responsibilities (if applicable)
- Duties/responsibilities (the how-to's are in the procedure manual)
- Qualifications (skills and abilities, education and experience, physical requirements)

Building a cohesive team is important as well. This is done through staff meetings and retreats. When people understand their role in the overall operation, they will have more engagement and buy-in. Think of your agency as a jigsaw puzzle. If you don't know what the finished picture looks like, it is much more difficult to put all the pieces together. The vision for the organization comes together easier when everyone understands their role and importance in the big picture.

As leader, one of your goals is to make the job experience pleasant and enjoyable for everyone on your team. When people are enjoying themselves, they tend to provide better client service. You want to create an environment of collaboration and harmony. By focusing on the mission and the clients, it is easier to achieve the annual goals and desired outcomes.

Keep in mind that people like to be recognized and know how they are doing. Providing feedback, informal and formal, is essential. While most agencies usually include formal recognition during the Annual Meeting, recognizing people's contributions and accomplishments on an ongoing basis will go a long way in building a dependable workforce.

You can demonstrate recognition and appreciation at any time in many different ways – and this needs to happen frequently. When people feel appreciated and acknowledged, they tend to go the extra mile for you. In the nonprofit world, it seems like there is always need for that extra mile! People are drawn to the nonprofit sector because they care, they are compassionate, and they want to make a difference. Remember, when you thank people and show appreciation, especially volunteers, it's like giving them a paycheck – an emotional deposit of goodwill.

While you are working hard to create a positive work environment, you still need to hold people accountable for their actions. Having an Annual Plan of Action and annual evaluations can serve multiple purposes.

When individuals and the agency as a whole have a written plan, as the Executive Director you are just the moderator and facilitator to ensure the agency is implementing the steps needed to achieve the strategic goals set by the Board of Directors. This also helps you see if any key actions are being forgotten or neglected, and you can make sure staff and volunteers take corrective actions to ensure everyone is carrying out all aspects of the Strategic Plan. You are the leader of the team that makes things happen.

When you have paid employees, your agency must meet and maintain certain legal requirements, both local and federal. You will want to develop and follow personnel policies and procedures for Board approval: you can find templates online. Creating a complete set of policies and procedures is a great way to engage volunteer support.

While you do not want the policies to tie your hands and make it difficult to do your job, you do want them to be thorough enough to avoid any legal actions. This is where your state association of nonprofits can be a resource for current requirements for your organization. Volunteers also need to have established, Board-approved policies and procedures.

Your agency can handle volunteer coordination in a variety of ways. Some organizations let each service area manage their own volunteers. Other organizations have a volunteer coordinator for the agency who assigns volunteers to the different service areas. The key is to have – and follow – a *Volunteer Policies and Procedures Manual*. Remember, recognition and appreciation are like paychecks and bonuses for your volunteers. When you are planning the year's activities and preparing the annual budget, be sure to include volunteer recognition and related expenses.

While paid staff will complete timesheets for documentation requirements, tracking volunteers' hours is just as important. Each year, the international nonprofit Points of Light determines the dollar value of a volunteer hour. Having a record of total volunteer hours – and the dollar value – to include in your Annual Report and funding requests can show the level of community support your agency receives. You may be able to use this information in a matching grant as well.

When you consider the area of human resources, remember the three R's – recruit, retain, and recognize. When you have a committed workforce that is appreciated the results can be amazing.

Programs and Services

In this chapter, we have addressed the organizational structure and leadership tips to build a committed team that achieves your agency's Strategic Plan. Next, let's look at programs and services. Clearly, programs and services will vary by organization and are defined by each organization's mission statement and bylaws.

Here is a list of questions to consider when it comes to service delivery:

- Do you have a clear definition of who your client is? Who you can and cannot serve?
- Do you have an application or registration process? If so, is it client friendly?
- How do you track the different stages of progression through your agency? (This is helpful when defining outcomes for grants.)
- How do you measure and monitor impact for your clients?

Use these questions to start thinking about what is important to your clients and your funding sources. When you have a clear focus on your mission, your ideal clients are easy to identify. This clarity will help to eliminate mission drift. Mission drift occurs when you expand services to qualify for funding rather than staying true to your defined mission. If you have a narrow focus of services, you will want to have a list of other resources to give people who do not fit your criteria.

Depending on the services you provide, having a way to identify your clients can help you track the clients' progression toward the desired outcome. The application or registration process is an excellent opportunity to get the release for liability and publicity. If all clients sign these forms when registering with your agency, you will know you have the proper documentation when you take the perfect picture for your website, social media, and printed materials. The decision to share photos of clients always takes sensitive privacy issues into consideration, of course. Based on your clientele, you may need bilingual materials and staff to assist with the completion of the form and service delivery.

While it may seem insignificant to track the different stages of the clients' progress, this can be valuable information for planning and funding purposes. An example of benchmarks might include:

- Number of inquiries about programs and services
- Number of applications submitted
- Number of clients accepted
- Client attendance or participation rate
- Program completion rate

This data can help you recognize where you can improve your service delivery. Perhaps you have more applications than you have spaces available in your program. This would be excellent information to have for grant proposals, so you can expand your service to support the community's needs.

When you are tracking program statistics for your Annual Report and funders, you need to take different measurements into consideration. The clearer your picture of the end results, the easier it is to create a vehicle to track that information. For example, you may want to know the number of people served by your agency (total and by program by different time periods), the different types of services provided (for example, the number of meals served, clients placed in housing, or jobs secured). You may want to track the hours invested in each client and the progress they are making toward the desired outcome. The more you can show effort to outcome, the better your story for funding.

Numerous agencies do an astounding job of service delivery, yet they lack the ability to tell their stories in numbers. Think of how those numbers can translate into fundraising dollars. Those dollars may be from individual donors, local businesses, corporations, or foundations. Those program numbers are your report to your stakeholders. They want to know they are getting a good return on their investment (ROI).

Financial Development and Community Relations

These two vital areas can determine the health of the organization. You can find excellent resources online, so for our discussion purposes this will be a brief overview. The focus is being sure you have systems and vehicles in place to track the data and collect the stories to effectively communicate your impact to the community and funding sources.

Developing and maintaining donor relationships are essential to your organization. Many times, an organization will go straight to the ask without developing the relationship first. Think of it as asking someone to marry you before you have gone on your first date. Relationships take time and are built on trust. The more accurate information you can provide in a timely manner, the more the donor will believe in your organization.

You want to maintain contact with your supporters before, during, and after the solicitation. This is especially important if you do not receive support on the first request. Think of it as building the relationship, so when the next opportunity occurs you will be top of mind, because you stayed engaged and showed appreciation for their consideration.

When you have special events, community happenings, and the Annual Meeting this is a perfect time to involve your special donors and potential supporters. Allow them to help celebrate the success they made possible through their donations.

Many grants require periodic reports and the final after-action report on a stated timeline. Be sure to honor those requests in a timely manner. Even if the funder has not asked for a specific report, it is a good gesture to send another thank-you letter with the details of the completed project. You want them to know they made a good investment in your organization.

Building community support is crucial as well. This may be in the form of partnerships and collaboration with other nonprofit organizations in your local community. In addition to having multiple resources for your clients, it can also allow you to participate in local community funding opportunities.

You may be a part of a national organization or association specifically created to help your target population. As mentioned, being involved in your local chamber of commerce or your state association of nonprofits can also be beneficial. This type of involvement keeps you aware of trends and potential threats and opportunities for your organization. You may even have access to resources and services at a reduced rate as part of your membership.

Always be on the lookout for additional resources for your clients and your organization. Plus, involvement in these external groups can improve your own knowledge and leadership skills.

Develop a Long-Term Strategic Plan

As the agency grows, you will want to develop a long-term Strategic Plan for the organization. Think about where you would like the organization to be in three to five years. If you are considering capital improvements, you want to develop a comprehensive master plan with phases. The long-term and comprehensive master plans are for more mature agencies.

Several different models of strategic planning are available, such as the traditional strategic planning model, the issue-based strategic planning model, the real-time strategic planning model, and the alignment strategic planning model. You will want to decide which method you want to use. As an Executive Director – and now as a Coach and Consultant – I have led several organizations through this process. If you're not sure where to start, I can provide insight and guidance.

In addition, it can be helpful to utilize an outside facilitator to manage this process, which can allow you as the Executive Director to be fully engaged. The strategic planning process can take three to six months (or more) from the beginning to the end when the Board approves the Strategic Plan.

One way to begin the strategic planning process involves conducting community interviews to learn how your agency is perceived and if the community needs additional services that fall within the scope of your mission. This is a way to collect data for the SWOT (Strengths, Weaknesses, Opportunities, and Threats) analysis for your organization. It is important to get input from multiple sources, including clients, program volunteers, staff, and Board members in addition to the community interviews.

When you are just starting out, keep it simple. What needs to be completed this year to meet the stated goals to carry out your mission? Working with the Board of Directors, what are the Five Key Area Outcomes that would move your agency forward? Identify a measurable outcome for each area. Just as a blueprint guides all activities to construct a house, the Strategic Plan guides all your agency's activities for the year (and possibly for the next three to five years).

Next, you will decide who is responsible for each action to ensure the project is complete. Going back to the house analogy, think of this as the different tradespeople doing their job according to the blueprint. The electrician will do the wiring, the plumber will install the water system, and different teams of workers will build and, eventually, paint the walls.

In the same way, the organization will achieve its goals for the year as long as someone is clearly responsible for the measurable outcomes for each of the Five Key Area Outcomes. In time, each team will have its Plan of Action (its own smaller "blueprint") that supports the Strategic Plan (the overall "blueprint") for the year.

The Annual Plan of Action is a clear picture of the expectations for each staff member or committee for the year and how they will support your agency's Strategic Plan. Take a moment to review the Annual Plan of Action template, which starts with a coversheet and includes an individual sheet for each objective listed in the Strategic Plan.

XYZ ORGANIZATION
ANNUAL PLAN OF ACTION COVERSHEET

Staff or Committee: _____ Year: _____

2024-2029 Long-Range Plan

1. *Organization's Five Key Target Areas from Strategic Plan*
2.
3.
4.
5. *Samples include Membership, Program, Image, Money, Management, Facilities*

Objectives: *(The number of objectives will vary depending on your goals)*

1. TO ...

   SO THAT ... (from Plan of Action Individual Objective sheet)

2. TO ...

   SO THAT ... (from Plan of Action Individual Objective sheet)

3. TO ...

   SO THAT ... (from Plan of Action Individual Objective sheet)

4. TO ...

   SO THAT ... (from Plan of Action Individual Objective sheet)

5, TO ...

   SO THAT ... (from Plan of Action Individual Objective sheet)

6. TO ...

   SO THAT ... (from Plan of Action Individual Objective sheet)

Review Dates:

Using the Annual Plan of Action template, every staff member or committee clearly indicates how they will support the Strategic Plan's Five Key Area Outcomes in their individual area of responsibility. Each staff member or committee will develop measurable outcomes they will focus on to stay on track for the year.

Here is a simple and easy-to-use format to clarify measurable objectives:

- To (state the action)
- So that (state the outcome)
- By (state the date)

For example: *To* train 50 facilitators *so that* 1,000 youth receive training in financial literacy *by* December 31, 2023. This statement is then followed by strategies to achieve the stated outcome.

The one-page Annual Plan of Action Coversheet reflects all the objectives for that individual or committee in an easy-to-read format with review dates at the bottom of the page.

In addition, each staff member or committee completes an Annual Plan of Action for *each* objective. Review the Annual Plan of Action template, and you will see a place to show current status, specific strategies to achieve that objective, the target date, and the completion date.

XYZ ORGANIZATION
ANNUAL PLAN OF ACTION
INDIVIDUAL OBJECTIVE

Staff or Committee: _____ Year: _____

Key Area of Responsibility: *(from job description)*

Current Status:

Objective: TO...

Desired Outcome/Results: SO THAT ...

(The individual Objective and Desired Results will be listed on the Annual Plan of Action Coversheet. The number of strategies depends on what is needed for the desired outcome.)

Strategies:	Target Date:	Completion Date:
1.		
2.		
3.		
4.		

In my tenure as an Executive Director, I found it helpful to have each staff member and committee complete an Annual Plan of Action to ensure we would meet the goals in the Strategic Plan. With each staff member or committee completing their own Annual Plan of Action supported by strategies for each objective, everyone had more ownership and commitment to achieve the Strategic Plan.

When you have an Annual Plan of Action, you always know your next step. You don't waste time talking about what to do next. Outside circumstances may cause the strategies to change, yet the overall objective will stay the same in most cases. This allows you to continue to move forward toward the stated goal. This gives staff, volunteers, and the various committees a sense of accomplishment as everyone makes progress toward the goal.

Action plans help simplify your organization, allowing you to focus on better ways to deliver services. It also helps when turnover occurs; new employees and volunteers know exactly what they need to complete for the year.

CONSIDER THESE GROWTH ACTION STEPS

Here are possible actions to grow your agency:

- Design or update your agency organizational chart.
- Develop or review job descriptions for accuracy.
- Develop or review personnel policies and procedures for paid and volunteer staff.
- Work with the Board of Directors to adopt the Five Key Area Outcomes for the year.
- Have every staff member and committee create an Annual Plan of Action based on the Five Key Area Outcomes. This includes adding strategies to their Annual Plan of Action for each objective listed on their coversheet.
- Establish measurements and a tracking system for program data.
- Determine a timely, thorough process to maintain donor records (individual and grants).
- Design your own action step.

MY GROWTH ACTION PLAN

ACTION	DUE BY	DONE

CHAPTER 5

Building Systems and Infrastructure

NO HOUSE WILL FUNCTION WITHOUT the different systems operating properly. Can you imagine living in a house without working indoor plumbing, operational heating and cooling units, and electricity for lights? Just like a house, your organization needs systems to run effectively and efficiently. All systems need to be fully operational with and without your presence.

Setting up systems can lighten the load. The acronym for SYSTEM says it all – Save Your Self Time Energy Money:

S = Save
Y = Your
S = Self
T = Time
E = Energy
M = Money

I like to say that the time you invest in setting up systems will repay you tenfold. If you find yourself doing repetitive actions, look for ways to streamline those tasks. When you invest in the development of a *Standard Operating Procedures (SOP) Manual*, you can refer people to the manual for instruction on how to complete a task, saving time and energy for everyone. You are creating a staff that can be self-sufficient, while you are utilizing your time and energy for other pressing matters.

Ask staff members and volunteers to make a video or write down the procedures for the different processes they are responsible for completing. This will lighten your load and give them ownership of the process.

Everyone needs to understand that the *SOP Manual* will strengthen the organization and allow everyone to have more time once the manual is complete. If staff members and volunteers don't understand the rationale behind the *SOP Manual*, it can create fear. You may need to reassure them that they are the experts in their jobs, and you are not looking to replace them. Your goal is to strengthen the foundation of the organization.

The *SOP Manual* can be a set of written documents or a series of videos stored on a central server or in the cloud. The manual captures routine procedures and processes, so everyone understands the rationale and method of operations. Either way, be sure you have a table of contents and/ or an index to find information quickly.

When you find yourself recreating a document, you may want to create a template. Having a set of templates can save you lots of time and frustration. Consider creating templates for:

- Board and committee agendas – these tie to the Board's Annual Plan of Action
- Board and committee minutes
- Checklist for events and event supply boxes

- Checklist for marketing materials
- Checklist for training events

What can you add to the list for documents that you create regularly?

In addition to creating time-saving templates, take a few minutes to put other time-saving items in place. For example, if your agency holds events or trainings offsite, you may want to gather a box of office supplies – pens, sticky notes, markers, scissors, tape, and so forth – that goes to every event. Other items might include extension cords, nametags, microphone, batteries, and flash drives. A detailed checklist with the supply box will remind you to include all items when packing up to ensure you don't forget anything. When you have a list, it is easy to ask someone else to gather the items, allowing you to focus on tasks and projects you can't delegate.

What if you thought "one and done"? Every time you do something that you know is going to be repeated, make a video or write down the steps and instructions and put this in the *SOP Manual*. As your staff grows, you can easily delegate the task with the goal of getting it done correctly. This can be a great incentive for staff members to think about as the agency grows. Ask them: "Who will do this job or function when we are able to promote you to Director (if that is in your Strategic Plan)?" When people have an invested interest in ensuring the future direction of the agency, incredible tenure and results can occur.

Financial Systems

Protecting the agency's assets is one of the key responsibilities of the Board and the Executive Director. Each month the agency must prepare its financial reports, which the Board of Directors or one of its committees must review, along with the Executive Director. The financial reports reflect what has happened. The budgeting process is to show what is projected. Having a good budgeting process can facilitate Board member's understanding of their fiduciary responsibilities to the agency.

Allowing adequate time to prepare and review the annual budget will generate a more realistic picture of the needed income and resources for the organization to carry out its mission. Depending on the size of your agency and the number of people involved, the length of time to develop the annual budget will vary.

Board and staff members working together create a stronger budget. The staff (remember this can be volunteer or paid) who work directly with the clientele will know the needed services and resources required to deliver those services. Be sure to gather data, when possible, to show justification for the needed resources. The Board members will be the champions for those services at the Board meeting when they review and vote on the annual budget.

As a first step, the organization will need to decide on the timing to begin the budgeting process. The budget may include individual program budgets that feed into the organizational budget. Remember to include both financial and in-kind donations in your annual budget.

Here are steps for the budgeting process:

- Determine timeline
- Agree on the goals – desired outcomes for the year
- Understand current financial status
- Agree on budget approach
- Develop draft expense budget
- Develop draft income budget
- Review draft total budget
- Approve annual budget
- Document budget decisions
- Implement budget

Be sure to include the budget process and timing on the Annual Master Calendar, so everyone is aware of the due dates and their responsibilities.

The nonprofit sector uses different terminology than the business sector. In the business world, profit is the driving force. In the nonprofit world, while the agency is run like a business it is not about making money – it is about delivering service.

Take a moment to review the comparison of nonprofit terms and for-profit business terms.

NONPROFIT TERMS	FOR-PROFIT BUSINESS TERMS
• Statement of Financial Position	• Balance Sheet
• Statement of Activities	• Profit & Loss (P&L) Statement
• Statement of Functional Expenses	• Expenses by Program
• Statement of Cash Flow	• Cash Flow

Understanding the business terms and the nonprofit terms will make it easier for you to communicate with the Board and committee members, since most of them will be coming from the business sector.

The Board will want to establish policies for financial issues to ensure checks and balances are in place. These may be reflected in the Chart of Approval for easy reference. Segregation of duties is an important aspect in the financial world, especially in the nonprofit sector. Nonprofits need to establish specific policies and procedures to protect the agency. For example: How will funds be deposited and by whom? Who can request funds and write checks? Who will do the recordkeeping and reporting? Check with your state association of nonprofits to learn the latest best practices for financial matters.

Having access to a Board member or CPA who is knowledgeable about accounting guidelines for nonprofits is critical to ensure you remain in compliance with your 501(c)(3) status. This would include acknowledging cash and in-kind donations. While you may have a system to track cash donations, do you have a system to track in-kind contributions? Tracking in-kind donations can be beneficial if you want to include this in a matching grant request.

Technology

Today we have the advantage of using technology to help streamline the operation of a nonprofit organization. You can find free or low-cost software tools and applications that can help you manage your organization. Check with associations where you have a membership for current resources and discounts that may be available.

When you review a software or platform, always look for ease of use and ongoing cost beyond the initial setup. When you start using any type of technological tool, remember to include the procedures in your *SOP Manual*, especially the login information. You don't want a staff member to leave and you cannot access your data because you don't know the login and password. It can be as simple as having everyone put their name and login in a sealed envelope and putting the envelopes in the safe. When staff members leave or are terminated, you must have access to their computer files and software tools.

If you are looking to purchase software, check with TechSoup. As of this writing, TechSoup offers current software and services at a reduced price to nonprofit organizations. Here is a sample of what's available at the time of publication:

- Microsoft Office
- Intuit QuickBooks
- Adobe Acrobat Pro

- Equipment
- Cloud services

When you are looking for computer support for program management, fundraising and grant management, as well as marketing you may want to check out Salesforce. Salesforce has been a leader in business software for years. It now has its own nonprofit division – Nonprofit Cloud. Check the company's website to see which programs are currently available. For example, at the time of this writing, the Nonprofit Success Pack includes the first ten subscriptions free as part of Salesforce's Power of Us Program. That software package includes tools for fundraising, marketing and engagement, program management, and grant management. Check their website to see if your agency is eligible for the free product.

Software and new platforms are continually being developed. Your state association of nonprofits or professional organizations may offer resources and best practices. If you use multiple venders for your software needs, make sure the different systems and databases will "talk" to one another. For example, if one of your volunteers is also a donor as well as a recipient of services, how will you avoid duplication when sending out mailings? This is where it is helpful to have access to IT professionals.

Managing the Board can be a challenge if you don't have a common drive or online portal. You may want to check out the online platforms specifically designed for nonprofit Boards of Directors. You can store Board profiles, agendas, minutes, your *Board Manual,* and other support documents in one place, ensuring all documents are easy to access. BoardSpot offers a grant program (90 percent off) to small nonprofits. You can get it for as little as $10 per month as of this writing. Check BoardSpot's website for a free trial and online demo.

I encourage you to check out new technology that may meet your specific needs. The key is to have general software for the agency, a method and system to track program and volunteer activities, as well as donor and grant management. Keeping your Board members informed with the current information and having a place where they can access the latest version of items can be a huge timesaver for you as the Executive Director. Technology needs to be your friend – it will help you save time, energy, and money.

By now, if you have been creating your Annual Master Calendar and yearly Board Calendar, you can see how you can spread out the workload to avoid last-minute crises and stress. Please do yourself and the agency a favor, and don't invite drama into your life by failing to plan. The Agency Master Calendar, yearly Board Calendar, and technology tools can be lifesavers.

Remember, your goal is a well-run agency with less stress and more fun. When you simplify, it is easier to serve more people and carry out your mission.

CONSIDER THESE GROWTH ACTION STEPS

Here are possible actions to grow your agency:

- Hold a meeting to set the tone for the importance and benefit of a *Standard Operating Procedures (SOP) Manual.*
- Create and/or review the *SOP Manual.*
- Develop needed templates for your organization.
- Define the budgeting process for your agency.
- Review policies and procedures to ensure separation of duties and adhere to policies.
- Establish how your agency will handle and record in-kind donations.
- Set up a system to accurately track volunteer hours.
- Conduct a technology assessment to determine unmet needs throughout your organization.
- Develop a plan to address your technology needs.
- Design your own action step.

MY GROWTH ACTION PLAN

ACTION	DUE BY	DONE

CHAPTER 6:

"Final Inspection" –
End-Of-Year Review and Audit

YOU HAVE BEEN BUILDING YOUR AGENCY throughout the year. Now it's time for the inspection, if we think in terms of building our strong house. You will want to know that your house is in order, so when the Big Bad Wolf (adversity) appears, you are ready. Your agency is strong and solid, with years of sustainability ahead.

You will want to review three different areas at the end of the year: an audit of the agency's financial position, program evaluation and achievements, and year-end performance reviews for your staff. This information can be the basis for the Annual Report and Annual Meeting.

Management Review or Full Audit

Depending on the size of your agency, you will need a management review or full audit of the agency's financial information. A management review shows that an outside, impartial CPA or audit firm has reviewed your accounting records. During a full audit, the auditor pulls the financial records to verify the accuracy of the financial statements. Sometimes, even if you could qualify for a management review, you can choose to have a full audit, so your organization can apply for certain grants.

As your agency grows, you may want to consider forming an Audit Committee as well as a Finance Committee. The Finance Committee is an internal Board committee that meets monthly to review the financial health of your agency and to oversee revenue and expenses. The Audit Committee focuses exclusively on the audit process. This group engages with the audit firm and receives the audit findings. It is one more check and balance to ensure the integrity of the organization, which you can promote to the public.

For the Executive Director a management review or full audit can be a moment of truth. If you have not been faithful in keeping the financial processes and documents "clean" and running the agency in a professional manner, this is where the rubber meets the road. However, if you have done an outstanding job of maintaining financial records, including donor records, this is a time you can shine. It is nice for the audit firm – an impartial third party – to recognize your efforts with the Board of Directors. It can be a vote of confidence in your leadership ability.

Although you manage your program numbers monthly, the end of the year is the time to capture the overall picture of your organization's impact on your clients. This information is key in preparing the Annual Report. The Annual Report is equivalent to a stockholder's report in the for-profit business world. You want the community and donors to know the difference your organization makes within the community and for your clients. Showing the progress from year to year can be very effective. Telling your clients' success stories with pictures can help you solicit future donations.

As you review your programs, this can be a time to evaluate each of them. Ask questions, such as:

- Does the community still need this program?
- What changes do we need to make?
- Is there a better way to deliver the service?
- Has the program outlived its usefulness?
- Could it be merged with another program?

Over time, program needs and focuses change. You want to be sure your programs are still within your mission statement and that you are effectively and efficiently delivering those services. Sometimes the program may still be needed but is no longer cost effective. As you propose changes, this is where using the Board Action Item Form can be beneficial.

Your audit and year-end financial reports are the basis for the IRS Form 990 (whichever version you use). When you submit your tax return, your financial statements are automatically available to GuideStar and Charity Navigator. You will want to update your program numbers and any other details that have changed on the appropriate website. You may choose to post the Annual Report on your agency website for the public to see, since it includes financial and program statistics for the year.

Year-End Performance Reviews

When you are reviewing your programs, this is an excellent time to conduct year-end performance reviews for your paid staff. If you have established key performance indicators (KPIs) or an Annual Plan of Action for each staff member, this will simplify year-end performance reviews, since everyone knows the expectations. Performance reviews are a tool to motivate and engage employees.

Nothing is more satisfying than telling employees they did a great job and reminding them of the impact they are making on the lives of their clients. If the Board has approved the annual budget for the following year, you can share any salary changes at this time as well.

If an employee is not upholding the responsibilities of the job, you need to address the issue immediately and not wait until year end. No one should be surprised at the annual review if you have maintained open communication with your staff. Documentation of the process is critical to avoid potential legal issues. Be sure both you and the staff member sign the annual performance review form acknowledging that you have discussed the annual performance review.

If the Board of Directors does not conduct an annual performance review for you as the Executive Director, you will want to write your own year-end report, listing the results and accomplishments you have achieved. By doing your own self-assessment of your achievements, you are more aware of your areas needing improvement. You can ask the Board for feedback if none is provided.

The Annual Meeting: Reflection, Celebration, and Recognition

Now that you've completed all the paperwork, it's time for the Annual Meeting. The Annual Meeting can serve multiple purposes. While your organization's bylaws require you to hold an Annual Meeting by a certain date to share financial data and program results, this can also be a time of celebration. Although there is a business component, the event can have a party or celebration atmosphere. Choosing a theme and creating the Annual Meeting around that theme can make it more fun and seem less like a business obligation.

The Annual Meeting is an excellent time to recognize incoming and outgoing Board members, volunteers, and staff members for their dedication to the organization. It is also an excellent time to thank donors and community partners and, of course, showcase your successes and achievements for the year.

It is a great time to reflect on the past year as you get ready to begin the cycle again. You will start with a new Master Annual Calendar and yearly Board Calendar as you hold your Board orientation and Board retreat.

Each year you complete the cycle, it will be easier and easier as you improve and streamline your operation. It truly is a "plan, do, and review" cycle. Remember to update your processes and procedures in your *Standard Operating Procedures Manual* as you grow.

CONSIDER THESE GROWTH ACTION STEPS

Here are possible actions to grow your agency:

- Appoint an Audit Committee or Board member to oversee the audit process.
- Ensure the Board of Directors signs and approves the audit engagement letter.
- Review personnel policies to ensure all managers and supervisors conduct annual reviews as required.
- Meet with a human resources professional if you need help with the annual performance reviews to ensure you follow the law.
- Complete written evaluations prior to meeting with staff for year-end reviews.
- Hold individual meetings with staff members to review and sign each person's annual performance review.
- Decide the date and location for the Annual Meeting.
- Work with a team to host the Annual Meeting. Determine the agenda, theme, awards, attendees, and so forth. Invite past, current, and prospective donors to the Annual Meeting, along with key community leaders.
- Design your own action step.

MY GROWTH ACTION PLAN

ACTION	DUE BY	DONE

CHAPTER 7

Continue to Build Capacity

JUST LIKE BUILDING AND MAINTAINING A HOUSE, building and leading a well-run nonprofit agency involves a surprising number of skills. Looking from the outside in, many people think, "How hard can it be to run a small nonprofit?" It takes time, energy, leadership skills, and a well-thought-out Strategic Plan, along with dedicated people to carry out the mission and necessary services.

Hopefully by implementing even a few of the suggested Growth Action Steps, this will help you build capacity for the organization and allow you to have less stress and more fun. The goal is for the agency to function with or without your presence, allowing everyone to have ownership and commitment to fulfill the organization's mission.

Remember the KEYS to Success

Here is one way to remember the KEYS to Success for a well-run nonprofit agency and keeping your sanity:

- **K**now what to do and when to do it
- **E**nergize others

- **Y**ou and your leadership
- **S**et up systems

Let's examine our KEYS to Success in more detail.

"K" is for knowing what to do and when to do it for yourself, the Board, and staff. This is where the Annual Master Calendar, yearly Board Calendar, Strategic Plan, and everyone's Annual Plan of Action come into play. When everyone has the same shared vision – with specific tasks to achieve clear goals and objectives – it is more difficult for drama to occur. Everyone can stay focused on the mission.

"E" is for energizing others. As the Executive Director, you play a pivotal role in motivating and recognizing your staff and volunteers. People want to help, and they want to be acknowledged for their contributions. When you show appreciation and recognition to the staff and volunteers, you unleash an amazing workforce to carry out the mission of the organization.

"Y" is for you and your leadership. I cannot express the importance of self-care enough. If you don't take care of yourself, you will not be able to manage the organization and accomplish the agency's mission and future vision. Your ability to adapt to the different situations is crucial. People will look to you for leadership, direction, energy, and enthusiasm.

"S" is for setting up systems. When you streamline processes and set up systems to ensure consistency and efficiency, you and the organization will run more smoothly. In addition, streamlined systems directly impact your ability to build capacity. Remember, SYSTEM means Save Your Self, Time, Energy, Money. For me, it meant my sanity!

Look for ways to utilize these KEYS to Success to help you have more confidence with less stress while building a solid agency. Remember, Simplify to Serve.

CONSIDER THESE GROWTH ACTION STEPS

Here are final actions to build the foundation for a strong agency that continues to build capacity:

- Implement the strategies you have learned in this book that resonate with you and your organization.
- Find a community of like-minded people for growth and support, such as your state association of nonprofits, an association specifically related to the population you serve, and other local or national organizations.
- Continue with professional development – find a coach or mentor, join a mastermind group, attend trainings, and so forth.
- Commit to rereading this book in a year, and celebrate the amazing progress you have made!
- Design your own action step.

MY GROWTH ACTION PLAN

ACTION	DUE BY	DONE

CHAPTER 8:

When Are You Ready to Move On?

CONGRATULATIONS ON COMPLETING THE YEAR as the Executive Director of your organization. Each year gets a little easier as you and the agency grow.

One way to ensure continuity is to develop a Strategic Plan for the organization. As the Executive Director, you will find yourself thinking about future programs and opportunities for growth. When you capture your vision and ideas in a long-term Strategic Plan, your dreams can live on beyond your tenure as the agency's leader. You can continue to have a positive, professional influence on the organization even after you move on!

However, if you find the agency is still struggling after multiple years, it may be time to consider other options. Perhaps a larger, similar organization would take your agency under its umbrella and handle your administrative functions, allowing you and your team to focus on the program responsibilities.

Another option is to merge with an agency that has a similar focus. Combining the efforts of two smaller agencies can create a stronger organization that can better serve the community. Think of the Three Little Pigs and how they all joined together in the strong house. With either of these options, you will want to ensure your missions align, and your operational philosophies are compatible.

Succession Planning: Board, Staff, and Key Volunteers

Let's hope the organization is thriving and ready to go to the next level. You will want to think about succession planning for both the Board and staff members—including yourself. As with any organization, your nonprofit will always experience some turnover. As staff members and key volunteers leave, you want to have a plan in place to handle those departures.

The known departures are easier to plan for, such as term limits for Board members, especially officers. In the back of your mind, be thinking, *Who would I like to be the next Board Chair or fill other key leadership positions?* This is the time to explore that person's interest level and start the training process, either formally or informally. Some organizations have a President-Elect position on the Board or a standing rule that the Vice President steps up to become the next President or Board Chair.

You will encounter turnover of program volunteers as well. People move away, lose interest in the program, or experience a change in circumstances. Be prepared and know what you will do when these events happen. Processes to consider:

- Do you have a way to say, "Thank you for your service"?
- Do you have documentation of their job duties, so you can readily fill that position?
- Can you fill the position informally, or does it require Board approval?

You will also need to think about staff succession planning. As your agency grows, you may find the need for department directors. Have you been training and grooming your existing staff to assume those leadership roles when needed? Someone can be an excellent case manager yet lack the skills to supervise employees and manage a department. Be sure you set up your staff members for success.

It is helpful to talk with each staff member and ask them where they would like to be in three to five years. Use this information to provide training and guidance, so they can reach their own vision for themselves. Their long-term goal may be stepping into your role as the Executive Director.

Where Do You Want to Be In Five Years?

Have you thought about what your life will look like in the next three – five – ten years? You may be content to grow and expand your current organization, implementing the goals and dreams you have envisioned for your agency. Or you may want to take what you have learned and try your hand in another organization where you can learn new skills, gain new experiences, and perhaps live in a different location.

If the perfect job comes along, you will want to be able to pursue your dreams without leaving your current agency in the lurch. When you groom your staff, you ideally will have someone who can step up as the Interim Executive Director until the agency can conduct an official search. The Board may select the Interim Executive Director as the new Executive Director. The key is to have a plan to ensure your hard work and effort will continue in your absence.

Each year, take time to reflect on your accomplishments and achievements, personally and professionally. What areas would you like to develop? How can you set aside time to work on these areas?

You need to continue to grow and nurture your professional life When you review your successes for the year, update your resume and your LinkedIn profile. You never know when someone will ask for a copy of your resume. You will want to put your best foot forward, and you cannot do so if you have a thrown-together resume. Who knows, the updated resume might even help you get that next grant for your current agency.

Remember the Three Little Pigs and the Big Bad Wolf from the beginning of this book? Well, let's look at the story now that you have a strong, solid organization:

- Your nonprofit status is *not* in jeopardy for noncompliance.
- A donor asks for detailed program outcomes that *are* readily available.
- A key staff or Board member leaves suddenly, and a contingency plan *is* in place.
- You're feeling confident with a constant focus on the mission, *and* you are having fun.

When you use and follow the Annual Master Calendar, you can be assured that you and your staff are filing reports in a timely manner to ensure the agency remains in compliance with the law.

Having a monthly and annual review system to track your program activities and outcomes gives you a method to meet the requirements of contributors without additional stress.

When you have succession plans in place for volunteers and staff, you will always know the processes to fill the vacancies.

With a written plan in place, everyone knows the expectations for reaching the goals for the year, and you can lead with confidence, knowing everyone is carrying out the mission of the agency.

You are amazing! The world and your clients need you. Assuredly, the Growth Action Steps fueled you. My hope is that you take care of yourself while building capacity in your organization by empowering others, following a shared Strategic Plan, and utilizing systems to be efficient and effective in delivering service to your clients! Remember, Simplify to Serve.

Never underestimate the power you have as the Executive Director. Many people depend on you and your leadership. By relying on your clarity and vision, you will stay focused on the mission and help clients in need.

Congratulations on undertaking one of the most challenging and demanding jobs there is! It can be the most rewarding and heart-warming experience you will ever have. Please keep up the good work and take care of yourself. Remember, your goal is to lead a well-run agency with less stress and more fun.

Thank you for what you do every day! You are making a difference!

About the Author

BACKED BY DECADES of experience as an Executive Director/CEO of multiple nonprofits, Cindy Walters, MSSW, ACNP guides Executive Directors to take their agencies to the next level. As a coach, consultant, and mentor, she shares proven strategies to build capacity, strengthen the organization's systems and procedures, and demonstrate results for clients and community. This enables nonprofits to increase fundraising, serve more clients, and increase their impact.

Cindy's unique skill set directly aligns with the needs of small nonprofits – those with a budget of less than $1 million. Her experience includes leadership roles at the American Cancer Society, American Red Cross, Camp Fire, Inc., Golden Key International Honour Society, and YWCA. As a former national trainer with the American Red Cross, she trained new Executive Directors. As a volunteer, she served on the Board of Directors for nonprofits in Texas and Colorado and is an active member of the local Rotary Club.

In addition to her hands-on experience as a nonprofit leader, she earned a graduate degree in social work planning and administration, which gives her the professional credential of MSSW. She is an Advanced Certified Nonprofit Professional (ACNP) through the Nonprofit Leadership Alliance and has completed several coaching programs.

Cindy supports Executive Directors through her coaching services and various courses, such as the Nonprofit Automated Edge. She also consults on special projects, such as Board retreats, strategic planning, and teambuilding workshops. Each service ensures Executive Directors gain the knowledge and confidence to be successful in their leadership roles, so they can build capacity and make a greater impact in their community.

Learn more about Cindy's coaching, consulting, and speaking services. Contact her at Nonprofit Success Network, www.NonprofitSuccessNetwork.com.

Bonus: Free Agency Assessment

How is your agency doing?

Your nonprofit strives to deliver quality services, raise the necessary funds, and adhere to best practices with a smooth-running operation. Yet there's always room for improvement.

How will you measure up?
Take a FREE Agency Assessment to find out!

Let's make your agency strong and build your confidence and credibility together.

To see how you are doing, go to
www.NonprofitSuccessNetwork.com
and download the Agency Assessment.

Building Together – Let's Stay Connected

When you read this book, what impacted you the most? What was your biggest takeaway for you personally and for your organization? Please let Cindy know the results that you experienced after reading *Simplify to Serve: A Blueprint to Lead a Well-Run Nonprofit without Losing Your Sanity.*

Here are three ways you can give feedback and share your successes:

- Post a picture of you with this book on Facebook or LinkedIn – This is a great way to promote your agency and share the impact this book made on you and your organization. Use hashtags **#Simplify2Serve** and **#SimplifytoServe.**
- Provide an Amazon review – When you purchase your book on Amazon and provide feedback, your review will show up as a verified review. Your review will impact future readers and their organizations.
- Email Cindy directly at Cindy@CindyWalters.com – Cindy loves to hear about how you are improving your organization and how this book helped you build capacity and confidence.

Cindy Walters
Nonprofit Success Network

Relationships ~ Systems ~ Resources

Helping nonprofits build for tomorrow with sustainability

www.NonprofitSuccessNetwork.com